The Death Of Traditional Marketing – A New Revolution Is Here:

Why Using Online Marketing Strategies Such As Email Marketing, Social Media, Blogs, Video Marketing and Press Releases Can Help Propel Your Business

Simon Thurston

The Death Of Traditional Marketing – A New Revolution Is Here:

Why Using Online Marketing Strategies Such As Email Marketing, Social Media, Blogs, Video Marketing and Press Releases Can Help Propel Your Business

Table of Contents

Dedication

This book is dedicated to my beautiful wife Kerrie, for believing in me, supporting me and enabling me to follow my dreams xxx

Preface

My wife gets asked all the time by friends and family members, exactly what it is her husband actually does, and to this day I'm still not sure that she fully knows what to say when she is asked. I think I've been called an internet or web marketing specialist, business growth consultant and everything in between.

This book is designed to give you an insight into the ammunition that you could be using tomorrow to become more visible, engage with more prospects and sell more of your products or services, regardless of the size of your business. The very same strategies you will read have helped companies in a host of different industries, from finance, food and beverage, pharmaceuticals and IT solutions – to sportswear, hospitality, retail and accountancy. And more besides.

As the title of this book suggests, there are marketing strategies available that have made it quicker, easier and less expensive for you to get in front of your prospects than at any time in history – and it's only going to become more popular and prominent. I firmly believe the online space is going to grow exponentially and radically change how we do business in the future.

One of the advantages that this new revolution can offer your business is that its strategies can be implemented very quickly. You may also be pleasantly surprised at just how easily you will see results for your business. And unlike some of the more traditional methods of advertising and marketing – such as billboards, TV and radio spots – they won't cost you and arm and a leg, either.

The savvy business owners are already embracing this shift. They have adapted their company's strategy accordingly, so that it incorporates this new revolution of marketing that works so effectively because it does not *interrupt* a prospect's day, it merely becomes a part of it – and this is one of the keys of its success. No one likes to be interrupted or overtly sold to.

This book is as much for those that have little or no prior knowledge of marketing, as those who may take a more hands on approach to marketing their business. I have kept marketing spiel to a bare minimum and it is written exactly how I would speak, so it should read in a conversational manner and be easy to understand.

Although some of the topics are covered in considerable detail, I have broken them down into bite size chunks, to make it easier for you to digest. In addition, you will notice the paragraphs are relatively short, so it is easy on the eye too.

Ultimately, I wanted to write a book that, regardless of your level of understanding of marketing, you could take it in, understand, and start implementing sound strategies immediately. After all, knowing and not doing is the same as not knowing.

So read on to find out how embracing the change and taking advantage of these marketing channels could help you propel your business to new levels. It's time to embrace a new revolution.

Section One:

Getting Your House In Order -

Right Message, Right Market, Right Media

The first three chapters of this book are going to focus on what I believe are the most important aspects, the cornerstones and key elements of marketing your business successfully.

These elements are overlooked by businesses at their peril. This is why I feel you should understand some of the fundamentals first, before you dive in to the specific strategies that appear later on in this book. It's the most logical way to learn and will provide you with the most benefit. Think of it as learning to walk before you can run. Unfortunately, most businesses try to run the one hundred metres in a world record time before they can walk!

Whether you're being found in the search engines by people searching online, marketing your products and services on Facebook or putting an advertisement in the Yellow Pages business directory, you are using what is known as 'channels' in which to market your business. A channel is an outlet, a means of communication or a medium that you can use to communicate your business's message, just as you would by using television or radio advertising, a billboard or by attending a networking event.

And this means the internet is no different. It is not the silver bullet that many believe it to be, but if used properly it is a channel that can help you reach your audience quickly, inexpensively (in many cases for free) and really help to get more eyeballs on your business and help it to grow.

So to begin with, let's look at what I believe are the key marketing foundations for you as a business owner: using the right message, which in turn enables you to reach the right market, and all of this achieved through the right media. Whilst you may feel tempted to skip this section because it may not appear 'sexy' enough, I would urge you not to do this. Once you understand these principles, the strategies that follow will have more relevance and context.

The first section in this book, which incorporates chapters one to three, will outline these three important foundations of what a successful marketing strategy needs. Without further adieu, let's crack on and learn about creating the right message.

Chapter One:

Right Message

Early on, whilst I was planning and researching for writing this book, it became apparent that these first three chapters would be the most logical place for me to start. This, despite knowing you would be dying to get into the key strategies you can apply to grow your business.

But this is the fatal error **most** businesses make, and I don't want you to fall into the same trap.

And more often than not, the scary part is that these very same businesses have no idea whatsoever that they are doing it so very wrong. They are blissfully unaware.

I see so many companies that practically copy each other (unintentionally or intentionally) in their marketing, to the point where in a double page spread of a business directory (under any category you'd care to choose) it would be hard to select which company you'd want to use.

So why is this? Well, if you look very closely, you may notice something that ordinarily you won't have thought of before. In fact, it may be that most of what you'll read in this book are insights that you have never realised or thought about before.

Look at many adverts for businesses in the same sector, particularly in something like the Yellow Pages (despite its declining popularity) and what do you find?... most convey the same message, which generally comprises of the following:

☐ Company name.

☐ Address.

☐ Telephone number.

☐ Some features of the company (yes features and not benefits)

☐ Perhaps some company history and a website address (although I have come across companies who have a website that have omitted it from their advertisement).

Go and see for yourself if you don't believe me, its quite astonishing. Pick up a copy of the Yellow Pages, a trade magazine or local newspaper and have a look.

What do you see? I would imagine that the vast majority

of advertisements are all delivering essentially the same message.

Sure, the contact details will be different and some of their features (once again a mistake which I will cover later) may be different, but why are the messages that most of the advertisements are conveying <u>not</u> different?

Even more worrying is that hard earned money has been paid to advertise in this way.

What You Should Be Doing

So what it is that you should be doing? Well, as the title of this chapter suggests, the first keystone to marketing your business effectively is to craft *the right message.*

Now achieving this is not a five-minute task and neither should *any* of your marketing efforts be treated this way – something else that I will cover later in this book – but neither is it an arduous task.

I am sure that you have heard of the expression "Failure to prepare is preparing to fail" and this is so very true in marketing your business. If you do not think it is a critical component of your business you may as well stop reading and close this book right now.

Ok, well it would seem you're still with me, so let's look at a great exercise that gets you in the zone of thinking in the right way about marketing your business. All I want you to do to begin with is to brainstorm the following two ideas:

☐ What are the benefits that you offer to your customers?

☐ What makes your company different to your competitors?

Notice that I make an obvious distinction that I have already alluded to in this chapter. You should be placing emphasis on the *benefits* that your company offers – the problems it solves and the solutions it provides its customers – not the *features*.

Benefits tell your audience exactly what your product or service will do for them and how it solves their most troublesome challenges. This type of approach allows your audience to visualise themselves using your product or service – an important psychological battle in differentiating yourself from your competitors. You want emotion, for people to feel your product or service.

If you're currently focusing more on features, you're not alone as I see many companies making this very same mistake. The good news for you is you can avoid making the same mistake again in the future.

The reason it's so important to highlight benefits is because features on their own do not enable your audience to fully understand how your product or service can help them. It's not as clear as it could and indeed should be. Your marketing needs to be 'personal', almost as if you are talking to your audience one-on-one, giving them a reason *why* they should buy. Features on their own do not give any relevance or any context to your audience.

Is Your Marketing FAB?

In my opinion, Features And Benefits (FAB) together can work well, but never just features in isolation. Have another look at those Yellow Pages advertisements and see how many features there are as opposed to how many benefits there are. You could soon be standing out amongst the crowd and the clutter.

So how many benefits do your products or services provide for your customers? Just to give you a little guidance, here are three classic mistakes that you will see in many advertisements, where features are used rather than benefits. You will see things like:

☐ Family run business

☐ Long established company

☐ Your local <insert profession/business here>

Indeed, all of the above might be relevant but they are only half of the equation. Yes, people might have a preference for using a family run business, but why? A more personal, attentive service, strong values, putting the customer first rather than solely profit margins. Think about how it adds value to your customers.

Many of us would probably prefer to deal with a long established company, but use this to your advantage and spell out why this benefits your customers. Perhaps you have a consistent track record, you're more trusted or experienced, or maybe you're well known in the industry and have testimonials to prove it. If you can convey to your customers why they should use you in simple terms without them having to really think about it, you'll be way ahead of your rivals, believe me.

The same rules apply to simply listing what services your business offers. You need to be thinking to yourself about the tangible benefit your customers will receive, as just listing a bunch of features is not good enough to survive in today's competitive business landscape.

So in the case of the first example above: family run business, you could say something like:

"A family run business for 25 years, highly qualified and experienced with many satisfied customers. We've encountered just about every situation that you can imagine, so you know you're in the safe hands of a professional company that ensures

15

your work is carried out to your complete satisfaction every time."

You could also get a little more creative and list out your benefits as bullet points or icons and give them a one-word name, such as 'trusted' and then have a little explanation to back that up.

Another Way To Stand Out From Your Competition

In a word: differentiation. Differentiation is a topic that I speak about in my DVD "The Seven Strategies For Effectively Marketing Your Business Online" and something I place enormous importance on.

Differentiation can allow you to stand out amongst your competitors, something that you absolutely want to be doing, particularly when competition is fierce and is likely to become more intense in the future. There is another, perhaps even more significant advantage to this too, which if applied correctly can allow you to charge more for your services than your competitors, and essentially (and ethically) steal business off them.

You may be very surprised to learn that price is not as important to most people as you may think. Excellent service, reliability, professionalism, being quick to respond, over-delivering and maintaining good, regular communication can

16

eliminate the need to focus on price. If you're focusing on price you're living dangerously and are only a price reduction from a competitor away from potentially going out of business.

The reason relying on price is like playing Russian roulette is because in the end there can only really be one winner, and unless you're Walmart or Tesco, it's unlikely to be you. Also, if you're selling at near rock bottom prices you are having to work so many times harder than you should be to make the same amount of profit. You'll also attract the **wrong** type of customers and an indifferent image as a business.

So being different, offering great service and delivering excellent value are all aspects that can make a huge difference to your business.

But what does it mean to be 'different?' It could be that you offer a number of select services over-and-above what your competitors provide. Perhaps you're known for exemplary after sales service. It might be that instead of offering a range of commodity services or products, you're adding value with bundles, special offers and outthinking your competition. All of these are great ways to rule out price as a barrier for customers.

Differentiation often starts with your company's USP (Unique Selling Proposition), and utilising it to the advantage of your business. A USP tells your target audience exactly why you are different from the other companies in your industry.

Once again, this is all about the benefits that your business provides for its customers. Although a USP should be themed around your top benefits it should also be specific and ideally, unique. If you do not have a unique benefit then you need to start thinking about what you could offer that separates you from the competition. Don't be disheartened if you do not have one or cannot immediately think of one, as USPs do not happen overnight and very often evolve rather than being invented or created. But being proactive and brainstorming can help start the process.

If your company already has a USP, you should be using it to maximum benefit and reaping the rewards that it can bring. Anything different or value added that separates your business from its rivals can most definitely give you an edge.

You may (or may not) be surprised to hear that many companies don't have or use a USP. And of the businesses that do, strictly speaking many are not actual USPs, but company slogans or a list of one or more benefits that some of their competitors are also offering.

If your company's USP is focused more on features rather than a benefits – or is the same benefit that some of your competitors are offering – then don't panic.

In fact, even if your company does not have a USP, do not fret. The good news for you is that this can be fixed.

And once you do address it, you will be amazed how having a USP can benefit your business. It is almost like a statement of intent from your company. With it you are laying down a marker for your competition, as well as telling your audience why you are different and why they should use you.

Considered possibly the most famous USP in marketing circles is the one offered by Domino's Pizza:

"Fresh, hot pizza delivered in 30 minutes or less, guaranteed."

It's a great USP for two reasons. Firstly, customers know that they will get their delivery in 30 minutes or less. And on top of that, there's a guarantee – so it shows the confidence of Domino's in making good on their promise – and if they don't – the pizza is on them, so there's no risk for the customer.

This is the type of message you should be aspiring for. A message that is so clear and so simple, everybody understands it and can see what's in it for them. It doesn't necessarily have to have a guarantee – you may not be in a position to offer one based on your industry, product or service – but your message must state *with clarity* what the benefit is, what problem you can solve or what solution you deliver.

Chapter Two:

Right Market

So we've looked at some ways to create the *right message*. But the right message is wasted if it falls upon deaf ears – in other words the wrong audience or market.

Regardless of what you may have been taught or believe, every company has a specific target market. Every company.

I consistently hear a common statement from business owners when I present them with the question "Who is your target market?" or "Who is your ideal customer?" The answer they invariably give is "Everyone". *Everyone?*

You cannot possibly appeal to everyone and trying to do so can be a huge and costly mistake. You may have a comprehensive range of products or services that may well appeal to different types of niche audiences. Collectively these different target markets may make up a considerable percentage of the population, but this is not the same. But you cannot be all things to all people and market your entire range to everyone. If you're doing this, you need to stop immediately.

Promoting your business in this way is like constantly throwing mud at a wall and waiting patiently to see what sticks and what doesn't. At some point some of the mud will stick, but an awful lot will hit the ground too, and this is bad news for you.

The reason this is bad news is because the mud you are throwing, including the mud that hits the ground, is *your* money. Money that could have been used to keep on a member of staff that you may have had to get rid of, or perhaps money that you can use to pay yourself that hard earned bonus you've been promising yourself, a holiday or even to expand the business.

It may that you need a new company vehicle, item of machinery or equipment. Worse still, it could be someone's wages you've had to delay paying due to a shortage of cash flow.

However, if business is going well, think how much better you could be doing by spending your marketing budget smartly, and in a more focused and targeted way. If you are currently not researching or focusing on your target audience, let me give you another analogy.

Implementing a marketing strategy that is targeting *everyone* is a bit like going on holiday without having a definite destination in mind, or a route planned, hotel booked or flights paid for. You have no idea where you're going or what your plan is. It's utter madness.

This type of approach most definitely falls into the 'failure to prepare' category. The other aspect is that it's really not that difficult to focus on niches either, and so having a plan and being focused is not only essential, it's something that you are more than capable of doing. It just requires a little thought, focus and planning. There really is no excuse for not doing this.

Ways In Which You Can Target The Right Market

There are different ways to target your market, and it begins by focusing your efforts more closely on those individuals who you believe are more likely to want to use your products or services. Perhaps the most effective place to start is by their demographics – your target customers' age range, sex, income, education, home ownership status and location – to name a few.

You don't necessarily have to target all of the above. Perhaps focus on three or four of these and give it your all. Once you have targeted these areas you can then move on to target another couple if it's appropriate, but do not try and do it all at once as you may find yourself getting overwhelmed.

Whilst this may sound like the type of strategy that 'other' businesses or 'bigger' businesses do, or perhaps something that you don't have the time for, think again. I know of many SMEs that understand the value of using this approach and so it is most definitely something you should dedicate time to.

In fact, once you get going, it doesn't take as long as you might think to formulate an effective and targeted strategy. And just think about the cost savings you could make and how they could be put back into your business. It's definitely a win-win situation for you and worth the small amount of effort involved.

As you read this, you may well already have a good idea what your target market is, based upon the existing customers that you have. If you keep a database or list of your current customers (hint: you SHOULD be), you might start thinking about grouping them logically based upon current factors – their income or age perhaps? This is an ideal way to get started and it will get you headed in the right direction.

Once you have been through your list of current clients, you can then begin to think about future clients and how you can start targeting them. You will of course already have an insight into what your target audience is, based upon the research and grouping of your existing customers. You simply have to go out there and find more of the same.

And once again, all it takes is a little work and effort on your part, but the results can be astonishingly successful when you do this correctly, so a little effort can go a long way. I cannot emphasise enough that the money and effort you'll be saving in the long run will more than outweigh the initial effort that you have to put in to this.

Let's quickly explore a demographic you *might* want to target: income. Do you think you and your team could focus on targeting the more wealthy areas in your town, city or region? Of course you could.

You Can Probably Start Doing This Right Now

If you know your local area well, you most likely already know where the more affluent areas are. If not, why not have someone from your team drive around to establish where the wealth could be – so big houses and luxury cars could be your first reference point. With the internet providing information at the click of a mouse, you could search estate agent sites to identify luxury property-rich areas.

You can also do a lot worse that by using mailing lists, another tool that can be very effective for identifying a target market. In the UK there are several reliable companies who provide this service, and they allow you to drill down to your target audience based on certain criteria and parameters.

Once you have selected the demographics to target, you need to find the appropriate means to contact them. You could use direct mail – a method that still works and which can deliver a good ROI (Return On Investment) if implemented correctly.

It's also important to realise that success comes from not just trying once and giving up because the uptake first time around was not what you'd hoped. Certainly in the direct mail arena there are creative strategies whereby your prospect could receive four, five or more mailings, and so the first mailing is merely the first piece of a larger puzzle. If the ROI is sufficient, why would you not contact them multiple times?

At this point in the book you are perhaps now looking at your business in a slightly different way. Hopefully you're now evaluating what the *benefits* of your products or services are, rather than focusing just on the features. This in turn allows you to create an unstoppable USP, and together with your company's benefits you can now create a message that has resonates and has impact.

You have also now found your ideal, target market by looking at your current clientele, as well as the aspirations of perhaps where your business would like to be in the future, or indeed where it *should* be. So with two out of three boxes already ticked, it is now time to look at the third and final aspect of getting your house in order – utilising the right media for your marketing strategy.

Chapter Three:

Right Media

Step three looks at the type of media you can use to market your business effectively. By now, you should have an idea as to who your target market is and what message(s) you want them to see or hear. Now you need to identify the appropriate channels for your message to reach its destination (your target market) with maximum efficiency and success.

As the main focus of this book is using the internet to improve engagement and direct the spotlight on your business, I will be going into greater depth about the tools you can use and how you can use them over the course of the next seven chapters of this book. The good news is I won't be bombarding you with lots of jargon and geek-speak. I'll explain strategies in simple terms that you will be able to start implementing immediately. This book assumes you have no prior in-depth knowledge of creating or implementing marketing strategies and will break things down into small chunks without all the long-winded terminology that sometimes exists in marketing.

Whilst the title of this book is *The Death Of Traditional Marketing – A New Revolution Is Here,* you may be surprised that I make reference to offline (non-internet) marketing strategies and tools. It is a little premature to think that all offline strategies are dying a death or are completely obsolete, and so the book's title is a little tongue in cheek. In fact there are many offline channels and strategies that still work very well. However, I believe the future of marketing lies primarily with the internet and it's certainly a cheaper (and in many cases free) medium to use, hence the book title.

These days most of us are what is referred to as 'time poor'. We all lead very busy lives and the internet has the advantage that it can be digested at home, at work and on the go with the increasing availability and convenience of wireless (WAP) enabled mobile phones and portable devices.

This makes the internet a potentially perfect route to reach a good percentage of your prospects, and whilst there are always going to be exceptions, in the main there are many out there researching and looking to buy your products and services online. I am sure there will always be a place for offline marketing, but the advertising landscape is most definitely changing and may never be the same as it once was.

This is simply down to the fact that more and more people are using technology on a day-to-day basis, and they are both comfortable and familiar with using the internet for doing things that just a few short years ago would not have involved any form of technology at all. In short, it's a sign of the times. As you now know, relevancy is key in marketing your business – from knowing what your target market is, what message to give them and *where* they are spending most of their time. In many cases, this is likely to be online.

How To Tell What Will Work And What Will Not

I firmly believe to consistently produce successful marketing campaigns requires measurement. If you are not measuring your marketing efforts, whatever they are, then you're essentially driving in the dark with no lights on. You have no idea where you're going and what's happening around you. Ultimately, what can be measured can be improved.

There are many businesses that have no *real* idea how successful their marketing is or isn't, because they do not know how to – or are unaware about the benefits of measuring it. If it's bringing in some sales, they're happy – but how do they *know* it was that specific method that produced results? From my experience, a scarily high percentage of business owners have no idea, or guess.

For those that guess, after I've drilled down further and ask more questions, it transpires they really don't know and so please do not make the same mistake, as this akin to committing business suicide.

If you are not measuring your marketing, then you have

no *real* idea what is going on. This means that you are either guessing or making unwise assumptions about what you think is working or not working.

One of the keys and a low risk, cost effective way to measure is to *test* first. If you are running an online campaign it's fairly easy to implement with many different software packages and systems that can tell you where a visitor, enquiry or sale has come from. One of them – Google Analytics – is free.

This is very powerful stuff and gives you tremendous insight into where you need to focus more of your time, what messages are working and what your target audience likes and doesn't like.

In the offline world there are several methods that work, and ideally you'll need the buy-in of your employees, as everyone needs to play their part in ensuring they know where enquiries and sales – whether by telephone, email, leaflets or face-to-face contact – have come from.

A popular offline method that has been used for years and still works today is to have a reference number as part of your advertisement that your prospect has to quote, often for an incentive, such as a initial discount. When the prospect quotes this reference number you can instantly tell which advertisement triggered the call.

I have come across several businesses that will ask the prospect where they saw the advertisement (rather than having a more accurate way of measuring), and whilst this is better than doing nothing, in my experience it is not as effective as a reference number or similar tactic. You are also reliant on your staff asking every time without fail where the enquiry has come from – which in my opinion does not sound as professional.

Additionally, using a reference number or an incentive gets the prospect to take action immediately. In times where we are inundated with thousands of commercial messages each day, anything that gets someone to take action immediately is a win for your business.

Another proven method in the offline world which is perhaps less common nowadays but can nevertheless be effective – especially in retail – is a coupon, which forms part of your advertisement. Working in a similar way to the reference number, your prospect must bring the coupon with them to your place of business, with the 'hook' being some type of relevant incentive based upon your type of business. Clearly this type of strategy is suited for print advertising such as newspapers and magazines, although I have seen it used online.

But for me, it's not overly congruent with the online world – a world designed to be quicker, faster and digital. And with newspapers and magazines slowly becoming less relevant as the internet starts to dominate, this method could well soon go the way of the dinosaurs.

Ultimately determining what type of marketing campaign you run with and which one you discard is dependent on testing them. Testing the responses, the number of sales and the ROI will enable you to assess what is working and what is not. Your success will also be amplified by your understanding and knowledge of your target customers, because this should influence *where* you start with your marketing strategy.

This is all about finding the right media for the audience. So if you were targeting ultra-wealthy prospects, you would need to know what they read, where they spend their time and what appeals to them. Understanding your target market and their desires and pain points is critical.

The same principal applies regardless of your target market, which is why a little research to start with can deliver significant result. You've also learned that the throwing mud or 'spray and pray' method – simply advertising either where everyone else does or where you *think* you should be advertising, isn't scientific, strategic or cost effective. If you're adopting this method, it could be costing you serious money.

In summary, I've covered the foundations of marketing to get you on the right track, whether online or offline. We're now going to move on to the main theme of this book, the emergence of online marketing – a channel that is changing the face of marketing and indeed many aspects of our lives and business, and a trend that I can only see increasing in the future.

Section Two:

A New Revolution Is

Upon Us

Whilst Section One of this book covers the foundations and core principles of sound, sensible and strategic marketing, Section Two is looks at how utilising the new tools of today can help your business even further.

The 'New Revolution' referred to in the title is a reference to how the internet has changed the playing field for businesses across the globe. It has quite literally transformed the road map of business, commerce and communication and I am sure that this will continue to evolve at an exponential rate in the future with technological advancements and new creations.

Before I get into specifics and discuss the key online strategies that could help your business, I want to make something absolutely crystal clear from the start. There is a myth that many intelligent business owners, people just like you and I still believe to this day. So what is it I hear you ask? What is this myth?...

The internet is NOT a magic, silver bullet that will magically send you a flood of leads for your business. There, I said it.

It's *just another* channel to market your business. That's it. It's *just* another medium, a route to your target audience that can be used to promote your business's products and services, just like using the Yellow Pages, your local newspaper, a billboard, the local Chamber of Commerce or any another networking event.

What the internet is however, is an extremely powerful and versatile tool that if used correctly, can have a tremendous effect on your business. It is also arguably the most transformational invention in human history. Since it first emerged as a mainstream technology in the early 1990s, it has changed everything – the way we work, the way we learn, interact and do business.

The cruel reality for many business owners is that they see the internet as a business saviour – a quick fix. These things do not exist, even in the 21st century and with the internet in full flow.

The fact of the matter is that if the internet is used strategically and as part of your overall marketing strategy, it can be one of the most powerful media available to business owners today. This is exactly why in the vast majority of cases it is advantageous for your business to have *some kind* of internet presence.

Notice I said *some kind*. Different industries, different products and services, and different niches will require different approaches.

But ultimately given that the online space is such as part of everyone's lives (and this will only increase) – whether you're operating in B2C or B2B, it's worth investing in even a modest online presence.

One Size Does Not Fit All

The type of the marketing channel you should use is directly related to the type of target market you have. So if you're in what's referred to as a 'mature market', that is to say a market where your target customer is of a baby boomer age (over 55), the internet may not be the most effective media to use. In this case, perhaps print advertising in appropriate publications would be a more relevant marketing channel to use.

Your products or services also greatly influence where and how you should market yourself. And in the case of a website, whether you need full functionality, shopping cart, payment processor facility and any other whistles and bells.

However, the emphasis should always be on your customers first and what's right for them.

You are likely to get more of a feel for whether a particular strategy or channel is right for your business over the course of ensuing chapters, which should help guide you in the right direction.

The reality is that sometimes you'll be right and sometimes you won't be, but you need to learn (fail) quickly. A particular project or campaign not going according to plan should be viewed as 'learning' rather than 'failing' – and we all go through it. The key is to start small – hence testing – and once you know something is working, you roll it out in full.

Establishing in quick fashion that something is not right for your business is perhaps just as critical as assessing whether something is going to work. This is also part of the art of being a successful business owner and if you can quickly grasp this, you'll be ahead of many of your competition.

As I have alluded to several times already, testing is the absolute key to being successful, and whilst it may not seem very 'sexy' it is something that can make or save you thousands – no exaggeration. By not testing different strategies you really are setting yourself up to fail, or at the very least you will have no clear understanding of what's working and what isn't.

Not doing so is such a gamble and when it comes to running a successful business, I prefer to have the deck stacked in my favour.

Chapter Four:

How Social Media Can Get You Closer To

Your Customers – And More

So I hereby present to you the first in a list of recommended online channels to take advantage of. Exhibit A is Social Media.

If you're unfamiliar with the term social media, allow me to explain. Social media simply refers to online media that enables (and also encourages) social interaction. This was something that until the dawn of what was termed by the internet fraternity as 'Web 2.0', was somewhat lacking from our online experience. We are now not only able to see and listen online, we can also interact, and I am going to tell you how this can be used to your advantage.

Our experiences online have very much changed in recent years, with the advent of sites such as Facebook, Myspace and Twitter to name but a few. These interactive, social media sites have not only given individuals the opportunity to interact more and more with their friends, family and acquaintances online, but it has enabled businesses to reach their potential customers in new and exciting ways.

Perhaps most importantly, the whole concept of social media enables you and *your business* to market to potential customers on *their* terms. So what do I mean by that, and why is it significant? Well, marketing on the internet in general, but perhaps specifically by using social media, fits in to a logical part of the daily activities for many of us, where browsing and catching up with friends, family and colleagues online rather than by picking the phone up and talking to them, is now the norm.

So the significance here is that you are not having to necessarily interrupt or stop people from doing what they would already be doing, you simply need to make your business more visible to them, and I am going to show you how to do exactly that. This is where leveraging the popularity of social networking sites can separate you from your competition, and have your target audience feel that you are not necessarily trying to force them to buy something from you.

Participating in social media has enabled the masses to enhance and increase their own personal 'database' of contacts, such is the ease at which it can be done. For the user, the advantage of these sites is that they allow you, more than ever before, to keep in contact with friends, family, old school friends - indeed whom ever you want to, and all at the click of a mouse.

It is both convenient and efficient for the vast majority of us that lead increasingly busy lives, and this in turn is great news for your business.

What makes social media so popular is the very reason it can be used to your advantage. If you have experience of any of the many social media sites that are scattered across the internet, you will notice that what frequently happens is that mini *communities* begin to develop within an individual's sphere of influence. They may have a community full of friends, family and work colleagues, and all of these segments of contacts will have their own different interests, tastes and opinions, and therein lies the potential opportunity.

If you couple that with an ideal environment; a website where a culture of social interaction, communication and trust occur on a regular basis, you can perhaps now start to visualise the opportunity that this could present to your business. In essence, the very thing that makes a social media site so appealing for participants can be the very thing that enables your business to gain more prospects, and eventually more customers.

Once again, I cannot emphasise enough the fact that these types of sites and channels for marketing your business to a potentially receptive audience sit perfectly with the way that many lead their increasingly busy lives today.

Because we are all so busy, we do not have time to necessarily stop what we are doing in order to be 'sold to'. Subtly dovetailing your marketing message within a medium that your target audience is already using – or engaging with them to solve a problem or answer a question – means it won't feel like an interruption at all, merely another aspect of the social media environment that they're engrossed in.

With many of us being time-poor these days, working longer hours, travelling further to get to work, or perhaps spending more time away from home, the internet has become the one constant medium that many of us can use to satisfy many aspects of our life.

One reason the internet is now becoming increasingly popular is because it can be accessed from pretty much anywhere on the planet. With laptop computers, palmtop computers and mobile phones with internet technology (WAP enabled phones) becoming more accessible and increasingly inexpensive, you can now be online 'on the go' in virtually any environment.

This in itself may be a huge help to you, as you can be communicating with employees and work colleagues, even family or friends, from a train or a taxi cab on journeys which would have previously been 'dead' time as little as 20 years ago.

So the internet provides convenience in our lives. What it can also do is provide *instant* information, and in an age when we want things done yesterday, that fits in just fine.

Do you have very little time to get to the bank, or even write cheques and post them for that matter? No problem, you can go online and do this. Do you want to book a holiday, but you're not able to get to the travel agent? Simple solution, book it online. Are you looking for a date or a possible relationship, or a last minute Christmas present, or some flowers for Mother's Day or to order a pizza?... I think you know the drill by now.

For many people, it's not only the reliance on this most efficient of technologies, but the convenience and simplification of tasks which makes the internet so appealing. It is no longer the future... it is very much the present.

But The Rules Have Now Changed

And so integrating your marketing campaigns into media and areas where people will see you, being visible to the masses, much the same as a billboard on a busy street, is what the internet allows you to achieve. The difference is however, that with marketing in general, the rules have now changed.

What has appropriately been coined by several marketing experts as 'interruption marketing' is no longer as effective as it once was. This is why in the main, television and radio advertising has been going through a tough time recently. The feedback I've seen is that it is no longer achieving the ROI it once did. One school of thought that may explain this is that if we as consumers are interrupted, for example in between television programmes, we can simply change channel as there's only two hundred others to choose from! Same with radio, too.

This very same reasoning is considered by some to be one of the factors that direct marketing is so lovingly known as 'junk mail' in many parts of the world. It is perceived as interruption marketing, and therefore unsuccessful. Once again however, it is all about being creative, and with direct mail this is no different.

First of all, very few realise that direct mail marketing can be unbelievably successful, even today. But I feel the mixed reputation it receives has a lot more to do with the fact that most companies that try it get it so wrong. Just like any other form of marketing, if it is not implemented correctly (and creatively) it is less likely to succeed.

Direct mail *can* be hugely powerful, not to mention profitable for any business. There are entire books that provide strategies, techniques and best practices for direct mail marketing. Despite some thinking it's a dying breed of marketing, it continues to yield profitable results, which is why companies quite rightly continue to use it. One thing remains constant however, and t hat is the rules of engagement have indeed changed and strategies must be adapted accordingly.

Anyway, I digress.

Despite the fact that the title of this book is focusing on traditional marketing pushing up daisies, as I mentioned before it is somewhat tongue in cheek (as many marketing purists would agree), as it is not so much that all traditional marketing has bitten the dust, rather that there are new, powerful and in some cases more appropriate ways to reach your target audience.

The new phenomenon in marketing parlance is what is known as 'permission marketing', which effectively means that simply just barging in and declaring your businesses' products and services to the world simply won't cut it any more.

This may have worked in the past, when consumers had less media choices, not to mention less product and service choices, but not any more. The new approach is now a more seamless, subtle and appropriate way of marketing, a far cry to what was perhaps undertaken in the *dark ages* of the 20th Century.

If The Viral Effect Kicks In – You Win

The very make up of social media sites could lend itself perfectly to your business. One of the main reasons for this is the sheer speed at which communication can happen. This speed can be used by you and could potentially see your company's marketing message passed from person to person in double quick time. In fact, it can spread just like a virus, hence the term 'viral' that is now common place in the marketing dictionary.

You will remember that I wrote about the essence and success of social media being the community feel. Where pockets or groups of like-minded people gather, talk and share ideas. Well, they can be accessed by your business, if done in the appropriate manner.

Just like in any residential neighbourhood around the world, a good customer experience from just one individual using your company's products or services can lead to word spreading quickly. The effect can be like wildfire as other community members get wind of their neighbour's experience.

Once again, all you are doing is using the natural make-up of social media to your advantage, as opinions (both good and bad), conversations, general news and the spreading of awareness and knowledge about all manner of issues, can take place in an instant. Do you think this may be worth tapping in to?

The way these sites operate means that this viral effect often comes in many different forms, not just words. Social media sites can accommodate photographs, videos and podcasts (audio, such as mp3) meaning you can easily publish and broadcast your views, thoughts and opinions to a wide array of people, both inside and outside of your community sphere.

With the ability for others to leave their own comments, thoughts and feedback, what started out as a small acorn can eventually (and very quickly) grow in to a large oak tree, and that's exactly what you want to happen, assuming that it's good news. More about the significance of that later.

I very briefly touched on what the meaning of the death of traditional marketing *really* meant, as there are still 'old' marketing principles that continue to work today, and will continue to work within the framework of 'the new revolution'. Social media sites are a prime example of this. Although, as far as the internet is concerned, social media is still a relatively new technology, the same 'old' core marketing values are still evident, and in this instance it's something called 'social proof'.

For decades if not centuries, one of the most successful ways to market any business has been by having referrals or recommendations. This is why having testimonials from your customers in a place where they are visible is a proven strategy. Whether it is on your website, in your brochure or at your business premises, you should always have testimonials on show because social proof – proof from others who have used or bought your product or service – is incredibly influential.

It is also not just exclusive to the B2C wither, as social recommendations and referrals from trusted parties work just as well in the B2B arena too. This can be leveraged by 'partnering' with businesses that sell products or services that compliment what you are selling, meaning they can refer their clients to you and vice versa, and that way you both benefit.

The fact is that as human beings, we are more likely to respect a recommendation from someone we trust. This makes for an extremely powerful tool and also rewards the businesses that provide a great product or service, backed up by fantastic customer and after sales service. If you can deliver on all three you're not only going to have satisfied customers, but potentially many more prospects knocking at your door, each wanting to become your next satisfied customer.

Equally, if you're a business that is at the completely opposite end of the quality and customer service spectrum, you're going to find bad news travelling rather more quickly. This will of course lead to a distinct lack of referrals and recommendations coming your way, complaints circulating to online world and your business suffering untold damage as a result.

An Example Of Success

With more choices available than ever before, great communication, wonderful service, a memorable experience and all the other things that customers want and expect is more important now than at any time in the past.

If you want to see a great, real life example of how the use of social proof is executed to the highest standard, then look nor further than Amazon. They have used this technique very effectively for many years now and they keep on making incremental improvements that enhance the whole buying experience.

A great deal of what they do is admired by me as a marketer as I can appreciate exactly what they are doing, as well as why they are doing it. They really have thought the whole buying process through and now you will find many other online companies mimicking (although using their own individual variations, tweaks and wrinkles) Amazon's 'system.'

Amazon have strategically mapped out every step that you as a consumer would take in order to buy from them, from choosing the product category, to selecting the product itself, right down to what happens when you reach their checkout and it is time to get your credit or debit card out.

What they have done is enable you to search for and find any product, whether it's a book, a camcorder, a vacuum cleaner or a sports bra, and allow you to see comments and reviews written by previous customers. They understand that the more informed you are and the more reviews you see from people like you, the more likely you are to buy a particular product. Cool eh?

This is an extremely powerful strategy as they are using

social proof to not only benefit you the consumer, but to benefit themselves as well. The reason it helps Amazon is they are seen to be completely impartial and transparent and have their customers' best interests at heart (which of course they do), and this is undoubtedly one of the pillars of the huge success that they have experienced.

They have ensured that their site is both informative and interactive, and in doing so they are able to gain more customer loyalty and add value to anyone that uses their site. Their hallmark is the creation of a unique shopping experience where you can view other people's opinions before committing to a purchase. Previously we would have had to ask the owner of the business for an *impartial* view of what to buy.

Now I am not suggesting for one minute that you should go ahead and replicate what Amazon has done to the letter, I am merely giving you an example of how powerful the concept of social media is and how it can be used to a businesses' advantage.

Amazon quickly realised and this is why it forms the backbone of their buying process. They know that buying a new product, and doing so online in particular is often a difficult task. There are so many choices available, and this applies to what you want to buy as well as where you will end up buying it from. So what they have done is to make life so much easier for you and in return you'll most likely use them for future purchases, too.

Oh, and there is also the possibility that based upon a great experience you will recommend Amazon to others too.

Once again, I am going to emphasise that this is not simply a tactic for the 'big boys' either, as it can have a huge impact on your business. This is why I recommend (if you have not already) you have all of your customer testimonials in a place where all of your visitors, prospects and customers will see them. They're extremely powerful – but must be genuine.

If you have a reception area, lobby, waiting room, meeting room, you should have your testimonials and photographs on the wall in a nice frame and ensure that they can be clearly and easily seen by everybody. All of these testimonials and photographs are like votes of confidence from people declaring that your company is great at what it does.

Believe me when I say that your prospects and clients will not see it as bragging, and neither should you. In fact most people like to be acknowledged, appreciated and thought of so highly. By having their very own words, views and opinions in a prominent place in your business, you will more than likely galvanise the relationship further and this will only encourage them to market your business to their friends and family. *Now* do you think it is worth it?

Better still, if you have a business where clear, tangible, visible results are part of what you provide to your clients (if you're a builder, DIY expert, mechanic etc), then why not have before-and-after photographs alongside your testimonials? This will provide visual proof and results of what you are capable of.

Some say a picture is worth a thousand words – and in this case, it's correct.

So to bring this chapter to a close, I would also like to just add one more string to this social media bow as it were, and suggest something to you that could quite possibly send your business global. If this is something that appeals to you, is relevant to your business, or is an option that's in your medium to long term vision, then consider the next three paragraphs below.

When I look at my Facebook profile at the time of writing this book, I can see that approximately one sixth of my friends are located overseas. Do you think that this may open up some possibilities for you in getting your product or service *international* exposure?

You bet it is.

Going global may not be on your agenda, yet. It may not necessarily be something that you have considered is right for your business at this moment in time, but the opportunity is most certainly there for the taking.

Not only that, potentially all it's going to cost you to have your product seen by a global audience is a small investment of time and a well planned and thought out strategy. But the pay off could be big, very big.

Social media may not necessarily be feasible for every business, it's just like any other form of marketing. However, it may just be the medium that takes your business to the next level, and who knows where that could lead?

Chapter Five:

The Podcasting Phenomenon. What Is It And How

Can You Use It To Enhance Your Business?

In my experience of speaking with and helping business owners, just the mere mention of the word *podcasting* generally produces one of two responses:

On the one hand I get plenty of "what exactly is podcasting?" from those who aren't necessarily geeks or as up to date with technology as others. It's understandable, given that it's still in its infancy as a mainstream medium.

On the other hand I hear something along the lines of "well it's the type of thing that other (larger) businesses do isn't it?"

In terms of the latter statement, they may actually be right, but that doesn't mean that it *has* to be that way. With the constant and continual advances in technology that we're seeing, the ability to produce a podcast has now become a fairly simplistic task. You certainly no longer necessarily need radio station or studio-quality recording equipment that has all manner of mixing software and other bells and whistles.

Just by using a good quality digital microphone and some very basic software, you can be up and running in literally minutes.

The overall view however, is still that this type of technology *must* be expensive, and perhaps explains why many businesses still aren't using podcasting. The truth is, it isn't. And in fact it is far simpler than you might think.

What Is A Podcast?

So lets look at exactly what a podcast is. To put it into its simplest terms, a podcast is essentially an audio clip (most range from 25 minutes to one hour) that can be embedded on your website and listened to. Alternatively, you can upload it to sites like YouTube and iTunes. From there, it can either be listened to, downloaded onto an mp3 media device, a computer or it can be subscribed to.

One reason why podcasting offers such potential for your business is because it enables the listener to digest your podcast at a convenient time and place to them, fitting in perfectly with the 'permission marketing' framework. In fact it could almost be described as a medium within a medium, as it can be accessed online, but the interested party is able to listen to your company's message wherever and whenever they want.

By using podcasting as part of your marketing strategy, you

are able to expose your business to another (potentially different) audience, an audience that prefers to *listen* to content rather than read it, and this is an important distinction. This is because as well as being listened to immediately, a podcast can also be subscribed to or downloaded. This gives your audience the choice to listen to your podcast exactly when and where your listener desires, and at any given time they choose. They can also listen to it again and again.

You Need To Give Them The Choice *They* Want

Having a choice like that fits in very well with the way a lot of us live our lives today, and is one reason why podcasts are as popular as they are. With seemingly so little time on our hands these days, you will see many people consuming all sorts of information on the go or in the background of what they are doing, whether at home or in the office.

If you're on the move it may simply be that you are listening to the stereo in your car, van or truck. You may be driving and listening to a music or an information CD. Whether you're on the go or not, items such as your mp3 player, laptop and mobile phone can also be used to consume information.

This demonstrates to you the sheer array of choices available today, because as well as choosing *when* you want to listen to something, you also have several choices of *how* you are going to listen to it too. And of course you should not lose sight of the fact that your target audience has these very same choices available to them too.

Podcasting gives you another weapon that you can use against your competitors, as it can allow you to drive customer loyalty too. By embracing a new way of communicating to existing clients, as well as reaching a potentially brand new audience, you have the opportunity to produce regular podcasts that your listeners will look forward to listening to or downloading.

If your listeners decide that what you've provided for them meets their needs you may find them subscribing to your podcasts, and then you've won an important battle in providing extra value and creating loyalty. It also means that they will be looking forward to your next episode.

Podcasting first became popular in 2005 with the launch of iTunes, and if statistics are to be believed, given the current trends in portable media device sales, as many as 275 million people worldwide will own a portable media player by the year 2011. This clearly demonstrates the popularity of listening on the move, or at least listening when it is convenient.

Audio content is also very easily accessible, and with the ever-growing popularity of iTunes, as well as the many other podcast sites that are available on the internet (and growing as we speak), those who like to download and subscribe to their favourite audio can readily search for and find content in an area that interests them, and that might just include your area of expertise or business.

This is why having your message in audio format can be so useful to your business. It is a highly used and easily accessible form of media, but there is also an altogether more profound reason for using it.

An Instant Credibility Creator

In my opinion, perhaps the most advantageous aspect of producing great, engaging and informative content via a podcast is what it can do for your positioning. By that I mean it allows you and your business to create a valuable identity as leaders in your field and sector, whilst enhancing your credibility to new levels. You could quickly become an authority in your industry.

I can guarantee that podcasting, building a brand, an identity and an authority is something that very few of your competitors would ever think of doing. This means that straight away you're more than a step ahead of them. Seriously, this is huge.

As far as adding maximum value for your listeners, why not interview your top customers and use the content of these interviews as extremely powerful tools for marketing your business – once again using the leverage of social proof.

You don't want the podcast to just sound like one big, prearranged flattery session about your product or service – it needs to be interesting, add value to the audience and keep them engaged to want to listen to the next episode. So make sure you structure the interview so that you cover the initial problem, how your solutions solved it, how long it took, etc. You could have your interviewee go into detail like a comprehensive case study of their experiences.

Either one of these options would work very well, and once again enables you to position yourself as an authority within your industry or sector. The bottom line is, it should add value to the listener and not simply be about overtly promoting your business.

With podcasting, you are not only able to engage with your audience by them listening to the entire interview, you could also offer a shorter version of your message, a preview or taster to pique their interest.

You may also be surprised at how just the intonation of your voice and what you are saying can add a lot of value to the way you and your business is perceived. As I mentioned briefly earlier in this chapter, some people just prefer listening than they do watching or reading, and so you're potentially capturing a part of the market that you would have otherwise missed out on. It's also very likely that your competitors aren't doing this.

The ability for your audience to actually be able to hear your voice, to get to know you, to listen to you explaining the features and benefits of your products or services in detail and with an air of expertise, confidence, authority and enthusiasm, can really help to build trust among your listeners. These very same listeners could of course be your very next customers.

Equally impactful for your business, once again on a number of fronts, is for you to contact leading names in your field or industry and ask them if they'd be happy to do a short interview with you, and have it recorded.

This Is How Easy It Can Be

Now before you think "well, they won't as they'll be too busy or because they've never heard of me before" let me give a real life example that I did for a client. In fact I must be honest when I say the ease at which I succeeded at doing this even surprised me! So there's no excuse for not doing this.

I was doing some work for a client who owns a horse racing website, and this operates as the 'shop front' for his own horse racing membership club which has a monthly subscription. In order to obtain some more profile for my client's business, I thought that it would be a great idea to do an interview with someone within the horse racing fraternity.

Ideally I wanted it to be someone pretty high profile as they would undoubtedly provide great content and of course their name would be known by virtually anyone interested in horse racing. So this is how I went about it:

First of all I researched who I felt would be the most credible and influential experts in the industry. From this research I now had a list of seven experts that I wanted to contact. I proceeded to contact these seven experts – all by email – to see if they would be happy to do an interview.

I made sure that I clearly defined the reasons why, explaining that the interview would also include an opportunity for them to promote their website, business interest, charity of their choice or something else that they felt would be relevant. This showed that we (me and my client) did not just want the PR to be one-sided and in our favour.

Seven Emails – Three Interviews

Out of the seven horse racing experts that I contacted by email, I actually received five replies, so this exercise achieved a more than 70 per cent response rate. From the five people that replied, I managed to get interviews with three of them.

So, overall as part of that project, seven emails generated three interviews. Total time spent including research was probably two hours. This was a great result, especially considering the effect it would have on my client's business, giving them instant association with some of the biggest names in the industry.

I can't name any of the expert's names unfortunately for reasons of confidentiality, but if you are from the UK or are a big UK horse racing fanatic from overseas you would certainly recognise all three of their names. They are all very prominent figures in the sport, with one of them being a successful horseracing trainer, whilst the other two are television presenters, so I saw this achievement as quite a coup.

What I am not trying to do here is show off in any way, I simply want to demonstrate that it can often be as simple as having the attitude of 'if you don't ask you don't get'.

None of the horse racing experts I contacted knew me from the next man in the street, but when approached in a polite manner they were more than willing to give me a little of their time. If you think about it, an exercise such as this can provide good PR for them too, so in effect it's a win-win situation, and that's one of the ways in which you can position it to someone, particularly if you encounter a degree of resistance from someone that you're trying to interview.

People Love To Talk

What I also found from interviewing these three individuals was that despite all being famous in their own right, they really are no different to you and I, except for the fact that as part of their job they get to appear on television.

I should also point out at this juncture that it doesn't necessarily need to be someone that fits into the celebrity bracket either. Undoubtedly the more well known the person you are interviewing, the better, but it does not mean that it has to be someone who is known from radio or television.

It may be that you could ask to do an interview with a similar or complimentary business in a different geographical area. You could interview an industry leader, someone who is considered to be an authority or an influencer in your sector, or someone who is well known in the local area that may not even be connected to your industry, but could be an influential character who is both well known and respected locally.

Interviewing anyone that fits into the categories above could have a major influence on your business, simply by the fact that you would then have an association with them.

You'll probably know from your own experience that most people love to talk about their experiences, their expertise and just generally about themselves. If you're anything like me, there must be several people that you know who will ramble on and on about what they've done this week, last week and last month. On this basis alone, you might be very surprised at just how easily you can find someone who'll be more than willing to do an interview with you.

By interviewing industry leaders, other experts in your field of expertise, or even authors who have contributed to books or publications that are relevant to your business, you may also find other doors opening, such is the domino effect that can occur. Something like this could have a profound effect on your business and raise the profile for the local area too. Who knows where this could lead in terms of publicity and recognition?

Once again I am going to mention the word credibility, and I am going to give you fair warning now, that this is a word that you're going to be reading quite a lot about in this book. For me, I truly believe that having credibility is one of the critical components in being really successful in whatever business it is that you are involved in. If you want to be successful or viewed as the leader in your industry, credibility is something that you absolutely must have.

Use The Influence Of Others For Your Benefit

There is something that you may or may not have heard of, and it is called credibility by association. Credibility by association is what happens when you're seen with, speak with or meet with a high profile name (possibly in your field of expertise, possibly not) and the general public get to know about it. This is where interviewing an accomplished, well known or influential individual can prove to be beneficial.

If there is sufficient interaction taking place between you and the individual concerned, and of course during an interview there would be, some of their credibility can rub off on you and this is exactly what you want. This is very effective, and is the way that many successful people around the world and in every industry imaginable have created their own credibility, and ultimately their own success.

So in summarising this chapter, try not to be mystified, intimidated or instantly dissuaded by the prospect of podcasting. You now know that it does not require a great deal of technical know-how to have an interview, or indeed any other piece of audio recorded. It does however, require you to take some action and this is something that I do not want to be a stumbling block for you.

Don't procrastinate over this, just go out there and do it and you'll feel a huge sense of accomplishment, and you might just enjoy it.

In fact, the two most common reasons people often leave podcasting well alone is that they just feel they do not have the necessary facilities – the recording studio, mixing system and other audio equipment – and the inclination. I would hope that you now realise you don't need all of this expensive equipment and all it requires is for you to grasp the nettle and take action.

What podcasting can provide you with is tremendous power that you can use to leverage the expertise, reputation and notoriety of leading people in your industry. This, even in isolation can only do good for your business.

Do you think that your prospects would prefer to do business with someone who is well known, respected and considered an expert in their field? Or would they rather deal with someone who is not particularly well known in the area or in their sector, potentially has similar expertise and credentials and is therefore just like the majority of other business owners in your sector? I think you know the honest answer to that question.

In the competitive world of business – as it is in nature – he who hesitates loses, and so you need to be constantly seeking to improve and remain at least one step ahead of your competition. This strategy could certainly help you achieve that.

Chapter Six:

Video May Have Killed The Radio Star, But

It Could Kill Your Competition Too

At this stage I want to point out that I am not simply plucking 'en vogue' or 'sexy' marketing strategies out of thin air – these are proven strategies that I have used for clients and my own business.

No doubt you are busy with everything that is involved with running your own business. Your day might consist of looking after your staff, dealing with customers, processing invoices, attending meetings and even thinking about your marketing strategy. I can't help you with the first four points, but hopefully the chapters in this book will shed some light and provide inspiration and motivation to pursue the fifth point with energy and enthusiasm.

Much like the strategy of podcasting covered in the previous chapter, the reaction that I often get to using video as a means of marketing a client's business is one of almost disbelief. It is not as difficult as you may think to create and implement videos into your marketing armoury, and this chapter will explain how you can use it to enhance engagement and increase sales.

The similarities between why businesses aren't using podcasting versus not implementing video are almost exactly the same. There is still a common misconception that using video is something that can only be afforded by, used by or only applies to the 'big boys' in business. That it requires Hollywood equipment and huge budgets.

This chapter will put that theory to the sword and reveal to you that it can be used to improve the visibility and credibility of your products or services. Video can really enhance your overall marketing message, and you'll also be able to have your company's videos ever-present on one of the most visited sites on the internet too, You Tube.

There's Good News, And Bad News

Despite some small businesses now (albeit slowly) realising that video marketing is an accessible marketing channel, for some reason they still aren't using it. As a relatively new concept, this may be due to the fact that they simply do not understand it or how to use it effectively. Although this may be true, I believe with advances in more mainstream technology this will not be the case forever. You should therefore act quickly to get a jump-start on your competition before they realise what video marketing can do for *their* business.

So at the moment it is not only good news for you, but it is bad news for your competition. I would hazard a guess that most of your competitors are unlikely to be using video or indeed any of the strategies in this book, so it's time to steal a march on them.

The concept of video marketing has grown in popularity hugely in recent years, principally due to substantial improvements and the greater availability of affordable technology. Camcorders are now relatively inexpensive to buy compared to what they cost when they were first launched, and this has allowed many more of us to film and upload our videos for all the world to see.

I first started to notice the emergence and increased availability of video marketing in around 2005 I think it was, and it all stemmed from the increasingly popular online home business niche.

The industry as a whole was already considered by some to be rather untrustworthy, and skepticism amongst the general public was rife. With both individuals and companies offering the likes of you and I the opportunity to work from home and make a good living, internet marketers now had a great tool that they could use to improve their reputation.

Video allowed the promoters of products ad services to demonstrate clear-cut and accurate proof that their particular business opportunity (or the one that they were promoting), was completely above board and legitimate. For those who embraced and used it, they had the near perfect antidote for those who doubted the legitimacy of their industry.

It also enabled them to become more transparent, which in many people's eyes earned them a lot more trust than before.

And therein lies the principal asset and the power of video marketing. It allows your business to fully capture the imagination of your prospective clients, be completely honest and transparent about the products and services that you are offering and fully engage with them. Video provides another touch-point for your audience and allows you to demonstrate in a few seconds on film, what it could take substantially longer to explain in audio or in print.

So now you can appreciate why video marketing is a powerful weapon to have in your armoury. Not only is it a medium that is widely accepted by many people (and likely to increase in the future), but there is the added benefit that your prospects are able to actually see you, your staff, and your products or services in action.

Lights, Camera ... Action

It gets even better too. You also do not need to be Steven Spielberg to produce an effective, informative video that will grab the interest and engage with your audience.

As is the case with podcasting, you merely need the basics in order to get yourself going – but most importantly it's about you – and your motivation to get out there and do it.

A few semi-pro tips: I do think that it's advisable to choose a location where the lighting is pretty good, and so if you're planning on filming indoors then a room with either plenty of light or light coloured walls (or both) is a good idea.

Sound is also something that you need to consider. Ideally you do not want any background noise if you can help it, as things such as loud traffic, noisy machinery and over enthusiastic staff could drown out your message.

And whilst you don't necessarily need to script what you're going to say, at least plan it and have a good idea so you can film it in a few takes as possible. But ultimately, be yourself. People buy people – so the rapport you build on camera will serve you.

That's really it. As you can see most (if not all) of it is plain common sense. Choose a well-lit area and try and keep background noise to a minimum. The great thing is that High Definition (HD) camcorder technology is such now that you can still produce excellent videos on a lot less than a Hollywood film budget, even with a tiny hand held device.

This May Surprise You

You certainly don't need a flashy set or a film or television crew to create a great video for your business, you really don't.

You only need to look at the videos that you can see on YouTube to see what I mean, as the quality of most homemade films is now more than acceptable for business purposes. Many of the videos you'll see have been created with simple, hand held devices and most of them will not even have been made with the use of a tripod or professional lighting.

I suppose the closest alternative to video marketing would be advertising on the television. The reality is however, that for many small and medium sized business owners, whether you're running a traditional 'bricks and mortar' or offline business, or an online business, the prospect of advertising on television is still pretty much out of reach financially.

Television advertising is still relatively expensive when compared to all other means of advertising, and there is no realistic way that many small business owners can possibly justify the cost of running a television advertisement. Even a simple 30-second advert could blow a company's entire marketing budget for 12 months in one fell swoop.

I believe there is however, a more fundamental and relevant factor at play here too. Undoubtedly there is the opportunity to reach a very wide audience in both number and demographics by utilising television advertising, and this is what television companies will use as leverage to justify the high costs. But just how do you track a TV advertising campaign's success accurately? It is very difficult to tell exactly how many viewers watched your advert. There are techniques that can be deployed but they're not used very often.

Most companies simply roll out a TV campaign for brand and product awareness with no real thought or consideration for how to measure its impact or effectiveness. In my opinion, they are only interested in making sure the message is heard or seen 'en masse', regardless of whether it is by their target audience or not. As you've already discovered, this breaks one of the key and fundamental principles of marketing – particularly as an SME where you don't have million-pound budgets to throw around – and that is: the right message to the right market is critical.

Realistically this type of marketing is only achievable from the bigger players in the market, for the simple fact that they are the only ones who have the type of marketing budget available to throw at such a campaign. As an SME your job is to out-think and out-smart the big boys, with creativity and resourcefulness rather than bankrupting yourself trying to compete for big money media – it's a game you'll never win.

Some Important Video Marketing Advice

It just goes to show how potentially flippant corporate businesses can be with their marketing spend, and why small businesses should never attempt to emulate them. Often TV advertising is solely about enhancing brand awareness or launching a new product. An established, big player in the market can (potentially) afford to do this.

And so for you, as an SME owner, it's about looking at other opportunities – opportunities like video. It's a powerful medium that has reach, is measurable and with more and more people short of time during their day, they are potentially more willing to watch two or three minutes of video than sit and read. Also, I'd add that it's easier to convey your personality via video than in text – another compelling reason to dust down your video camera and give it an airing.

I've already touched on this briefly before, but below is a more comprehensive pointers on how to execute a great video for your target audience:

- Choose a light and airy location, particularly if filming indoors.

- Ensure there is no background noise coming from an adjacent location.

- Plan in advance what you want to say. You could script it but it's not necessary – the key is for it to look natural.

- Try and keep the video dynamic and quick paced, so two minutes is good – particularly when you're first getting started.

- Speak clearly and focus on the message you want to convey to your audience.

- Ensure you have a professional ending to your video. I suggest that you use some kind of call to action: stay tuned for our next video, watch out for more tips coming soon, etc.

The reason I believe video works so well is it's more of a reflection of who you really are — it's genuine — and in many ways it's also more persuasive. It caters to our brain's visual and auditory senses, and allows us to recognise body language and facial expressions.

It has also become an essential and distinguishing factor for large corporate businesses, as they realize the potential, impact and reach of video marketing. YouTube channels are appearing left, right and centre.

SMEs are lagging behind however, and do not yet fully understand the value that video marketing can deliver. This is great news for your business and by the end of this chapter you will not only have a clear understanding as to why it can help you – but how you can go away and implement it tomorrow.

One of the key drivers to the success of video marketing is the success and popularity of the YouTube website. This has seen a number of other video sites emerge, however YouTube remains the most popular. In fact, such was YouTube's success that in October 2006, internet giant Google saw fit to purchase the site for a reported $1.65 billion. Yes, billion with a 'b'!

According to a service called Alexa, in 2008, YouTube was the second most visited site in the world, getting 60 million unique views per month. Alexa is a well-respected source of online information that has built an unrivaled source of website data, including visitor statistics, related links and much more.

Given these facts, do you think it may be beneficial to your business to have a presence on a site that has 15 million visitors each and every week?

Value For Your Clients Creates Wealth For You

In much the same way as you read in Chapter Three about social media changing the marketing landscape by providing an interactive forum for you and your audience, YouTube presents a similar opportunity. Not only are your videos online for everyone to see, gain value from and start a 'relationship' with you, they can comment on, share and subscribe to your videos.

While we're on the subject of creating value, I should elaborate on what this could mean for your business, you might be thinking that all this creating content stuff is a bit labour intensive and not really worthwhile. Think again.

Delivering and sharing value for your clients, for free, is an extremely powerful way to start building a following. Imagine if you just spent five hours a week – one per day – producing some video content, one podcast and some social media engagement. What difference could that make to your business in six months time? Of course it does require a little effort on your part – everything does – but the end result of your efforts could be massive in terms of differentiating yourself against your competitors and sales growth.

In addition, you will be building something even more valuable... trust. Not sure you can put a price on that.

Do you think prospects are more likely to want to do business with something they know, like and trust? Who they see and hear on a regular basis? Someone who appears to know all the industry experts? You bet.

In terms of your perception in the eyes of your customers and your rivals, it's all good so far. You're differentiating yourself from your competition, you're offering more value than your competition, you're seen as the authority figure by your prospects and customers. Do your competitors really stand a chance?

It gets better too.

Through the trust you've built, you may find your new audience – regardless of whether they are a customer yet or not – recommending you to friends and family. Referrals like this are possibly the most powerful way to attract business (plus they're free). Granted, the recommendation may not being life as a business relationship – they may just tune in to your videos, podcasts or interact with you on social media. But then the cycle starts all over again.

You've Heard The Saying "Knowledge Is Power"

By getting closer to your audience and engaging with them, you will begin to find out more about them. This information could be a powerful asset to have.

It may provide you with key insights that enable you to develop your range of products or services to meet a need that you had overlooked or didn't realise existed have. Suddenly, you will be gathering critical information that allows you to serve your customers in the best way you can.

If you feel you can't expand your current range of products or services currently, perhaps due to space, manpower or investment, why not partner with another company that can provide the product or service, and that way it's a win-win-win. They could also return the favour, and so imagine what this alone could do to your bottom line.

Thinking and working smartly like this will not only put you light-years ahead of your contemporaries, it will make you more profitable. You'll be creating opportunities in areas you never dreamed of or considered, and by differentiating yourself you may find you can start to charge a premium price for the added value you're delivering.

Price Will No Longer Matter To Your Clients

This type of positioning can put your business in the wonderful situation where price is no longer an issue for your customers. Do you think every customer buys solely on price? Wrong? You only have to look at what we can pay for a cup of coffee or a sandwich these days to realise that there are often more important considerations for a customer. Experience, prestige, feel-good factor ... just some of the ways you can combat the price issue.

This is a critical advantage for your business, because as I alluded to previously, there is generally only one winner in the price-war stakes. It's impossible for everyone to offer the lowest price (and why would you want to compete with the 'bottom feeders' anyway?) and this means that unless you're one of the major powerhouses in your industry or a company that focuses on volume more than delivering value and experience – you're not going to win.

By niching yourself, your value proposition to your customers becomes clearer. You will be known as a specialist in XYZ area – elevating your brand, your positioning and your notoriety. And with it, you will find you have the opportunity to increase prices, revenue and profit.

You only need to look at the medical profession. General Practitioners (GPs) can command what many would say is a pretty decent salary, but how do they compare with specialists? Specialists can earn up to three, four, sometimes ten times that of a GP. So now do you see the difference?

Video marketing could certainly help you on this journey to delivering a new value added strategy – and in many ways it could result in a change of identity for you. From simply 'Accountant' to 'Accountant that helps start-ups in the tech industry to grow and scale up.'

Video is only one piece of the pie of course, but can you now appreciate the impact it could be having on your business, and how you could be leaving your competitors in your wake?

This approach may go against everything you've been taught, heard or believe in business. That you need to please everyone, that the more clients you can target the better, and that if you raise your prices you will scare off all your customers.

Also, from a young age we're conditioned to believe 'different' as the one thing you must not be. No, instead we've been taught we need to fit in, be like everyone else and to not stand out because it can get you into trouble. Being different at school often has a stigma attached to it, and I am sure that we can all remember someone at school who was thought of as 'different'.

But being different in a business context can be the difference between doing ok and hanging in there, and achieving huge success year after year. If you're being compared to several (or more) very similar looking businesses, one of the ways a potential client may try to distinguish between the group is price – because in essence you all look the same – ie: you're essentially a commodity. But now you know what to do, and once you've read Chapter Seven, you'll have yet more insight to help you achieve this... and more.

Chapter Seven:

Gain Instant Authority By Using Article

Marketing For Your Business

You've already seen extremely valuable marketing strategies that communicate your company's message via audio (podcasting) and visual (video marketing) technology. Now we are going to explore another strategy that I have used with great success and this involves writing. Sounds daunting, right? It isn't, I assure you.

In simple terms, article marketing is an easy to implement strategy of using material – anywhere from 350-700 words or more – written about your area of expertise, industry or range of products or services. In fact, articles can be written about anything relevant to your business, however they should ideally never be too 'salesy' – the emphasis is on information and education.

Before you start thinking that you do not have time to sit down and think about what to write about, think again. You probably have relevant information stored everywhere in your office, something I'll elaborate more on this later

You have undoubtedly seen many articles in trade publications, local newspapers or magazines – and you may have written or had written such articles for your business. They should inform first – offer an educational perspective – and highlight your company and its features and benefits second.

Article marketing is essentially the same, but rather than writing for print publications, you're growing your online footprint, which will in turn enhance your credibility. So, how do you get started?

Well, because this is all about creating an online impact – which is both inexpensive and going to serve you long into the future – you won't be targeting any of your industry's offline publications. You'll be using what are known as article directories – essentially huge databases or libraries of articles that cover practically every subject and topic imaginable.

One of the key benefits for you is that most article directories are well respected by the search engines, the likes of Google, Yahoo and Bing (formerly MSN Search). This enables you to leverage your business on the back of their online authority, and improve your chances of your articles being seen by your audience.

There are dozens of these sites, such as Ezine Articles, Buzzle and Hubpages, and all can help you enhance your online reputation and get more eyeballs on your brand(s).

You are effectively scattering your company's name across a variety of quality locations, like seeds across a wide stretch of fertile land.

Another Massive Benefit For Your Business

As you've already discovered in previous chapters, online strategies often have a double-edged sword effect, and article marketing is no different.

As you know, information can travel very quickly across the internet, and as well as spreading your company's name, credentials and its proficiency across the landscape of the world wide web, there is another massive advantage to using this strategy:

Authenticity and authority.

Additionally, from a search engine optimisation (SEO) perspective, article marketing doesn't just provide valuable links back to your site – they are links from high reputation websites – and this is considered a huge 'thumbs up' as far as the search engines are concerned. The links simply come from your business biography at the end of the article, and so there is no mystical power or force at work here, you are merely using leverage once again.

These links are known in the internet marketing trade as 'back links' – a term that you may or may not be familiar with. Regardless, these links can have an massive effect on your company's website and its ranking in the search engines, as being on page one for certain phrases and search terms is where you ultimately want to be.

The whole concept of article marketing is considered to be on the most efficient ways to generate authority and visibility for your business. One reason is that once your articles have been submitted to the relevant directory sites, they are normally visible very quickly. In fact, in some cases I have had some articles visible in a matter of hours.

Do You Like (Near) Instant Results?

You would also be surprised at how quickly this strategy can be implemented. Do you remember that I mentioned earlier in this chapter that you might be thinking that you either wouldn't want to sit down and write a dozen articles, or that you would not be able to think of what you could write in one article, let alone a dozen. Well, it is not as difficult as you may think it is.

This is because you've probably got reams of quality, relevant information sitting somewhere in your business that could be put to great use. It could be on your computer, or a member of staff's computer, or in a file somewhere. Wherever it is hiding, it is an asset that you can put to better use.

82

A little bit of effort and planning is all that's required. The bottom line is that as long as an article is your work and has not just been blatantly copied or plagiarised from another source, there is no reason why it cannot be used.

There are certain key tactics that can also improve the visibility of your article, such as the headline. The headline should be relevant to the content of the article, but also grab immediate attention, as you not only want the article to stand out amongst other articles, but you want it to be read. You could have the most informative article ever written, but if the headline isn't compelling and doesn't convince your audience to read it, then your article is essentially useless.

Another piece of advice I want to share is that your article should not 'sell' anything, as this goes against the terms and conditions of most (if not all) of these article submission sites. And anyway, as you now know, the idea behind many of these strategies is to educate and add value to your audience and then they'll come to you as the authority in your industry. So there's no need for the hard sell. Once they seek you out and arrive at your website, this is where you can do the selling.

Be Different By Being Different

By now I am sure that you have realised that I really do stress the impact that *credibility* can have on a business, and I did warn you that I would be mentioning it constantly throughout this. I believe it really is *that* important. As you'll no doubt know from your own personal experience, all business sectors, whether you're involved in business-to-business (B2B) or business-to-consumer (B2C), are highly competitive – it really is dog eat dog at the moment – and as the internet advances, it will only become more so.

Most experts I've spoken to believe that even once the economic downturn that we're experiencing at the moment subsides, competition will still be as intense, maybe worse. I happen to agree with them – especially with online set to dominate the marketing landscape. This makes it critical for you to gain any advantage you can over your competitors – like now!

And one way this can be achieved is through credibility. As you've already read, it's not as difficult as many believe it to be, assuming that you're at least competent at what you do, which I am sure you are. Once obtained, credibility is a very powerful asset for your business.

What impact would it have on your business if your audience types in a search in Google, Yahoo! or Bing, and multiple listings appeared from a variety of credible sources and websites – all with your name or business name? Do you think they may be reassured that your business is potentially the one that they'd like to be involved with?

When I talk about credibility and the correct positioning of both you and your business, this is what I mean. Your online footprint is not only important, it can stay online forever. Therefore what comes up when people search is absolutely key.

Having a presence and an authority about your business could be a real game-changer. You've most likely heard it many times but perception really *is* reality. If you can get these key aspects in place they will form the solid, sound foundation to your empire from which everything else is built on.

Chapter Eight:

Why A Business Blog?

You may or may not know exactly what a blog is or what it can be used for, but don't worry, I'll be quickly and easily explaining the concept to you. It really isn't that complicated.

A blog (an abbreviation of the term web log) is a type of website that is generally created, maintained and operated by an individual person, rather than a business. A blog comprises of regular entries that more often than not appear in date order, and so think of it as being similar to a diary or a journal.

Most blogs tend to be written about a specific subject, area of interest or a particular topic, with each entry (known as a post or blog entry) ranging anywhere from 50 words and upwards. Blogs by their very nature are dynamic websites, meaning they are often constantly being updated with new information, which is one way (hint) they can generate a following. In terms of how often they can be or should be updated, that is down to the owner.

It could be daily, three times a week, weekly, fortnightly, or monthly. But consistency is the key, in my opinion.

Whilst the whole idea of a blog may have originated as more about an *individual's* thoughts, opinions and views about something that they feel passionate about, it is now a great tool that can be utilised by any business. After all – you're an individual – and what you would be writing (blogging) about are your areas of interest and expertise. And once again, the emphasis is on adding value to your readers.

Although the concept of a business blog is still very much in its infancy, I am starting to see more and more using them, and as the internet grows I believe this means of 'marketing' will also grow exponentially.

Easy To Use, Operate And Maintain

From a blogger's (your) point of view, perhaps one reason for their popularity is that they can be created and maintained with absolute ease. There are numerous (free) online tools that allow you to get up and running with a blog online in literally minutes. You can also easily include audio or video, and you have already read about the benefits of using these tools in previous chapters.

From a reader's point of view, a great blog is one that delivers regular, compelling and relevant content. Much the same as your podcast or YouTube channel, your blog can generate a following, with readers being notified every time you update your blog.

A good friend of mine, Gareth Harries, travelled around the world during an entertaining and interesting 11 months that were spread over the course of 2008 and 2009. He decided to create a blog about his trip, having never created one before.

For him, it was very much uncharted territory, in almost every sense of the word. Despite the fact that he was pretty much brand new to the concept of blogging, he explained to me just how easy it was to create his blog, not to mention how much fun and satisfaction it provided him with too.

The entertaining posts and entries that he made gave colourful and detailed descriptions about the various worldwide destinations that he had visited during his epic journey. In fact, over the course of the entire trip Gareth managed to visit more than 130 countries!

If you take a look at the blog he created for his adventure (www.travelblog.org/Bloggers/GWK1/) you will see updates on the many wonderful experiences that he had during his world tour. He was able to experience many things, from seeing tigers, gibbons and orangutans in the wild, to raising money for the less fortunate in Brazil by selling T-shirts. It was quite a trip.

What his blog also enabled him to do was to upload many beautiful photographs, which gave his readers and followers the feeling of almost being part of his adventure. I should also point out that when you factor in to this whole, epic trip that there were many destinations where the quality of the internet connection was not quite as we are used to in the Western world, you can appreciate and begin to understand just how easy a strategy this is to implement.

There is no excuse for not doing this.

By now you should be starting to develop a real insight in to how you can start using online strategies more effectively in your business. That social media can help drive engagement and spread your brand, how video can help generate trust and why podcasting is perfect for increasing your profile. And that ultimately, all three enable you to add enormous value to your audience in a way that only 10 years ago would not have been possible.

Interaction Can Lead To Positive Action

And of course in this chapter, you're gaining more clarity on the concept of blogging and that it isn't actually as difficult as you may have first thought.

Blogging is another great way to gain a following, and whilst it's certainly become en vogue with all manner of personalities; everyone from rock, pop and rap stars and NFL players, to Hollywood actors, retired singers and millionaire entrepreneurs – you don't need to be high profile to begin with to have success with blogging. As with all of these tactics – and in fact and business strategy or anything in life – it's all about getting started and taking action.

Just like video marketing, blogging was something that the internet marketing industry began using early on to establish their credentials as experts in their field. Often the pioneers of creative marketing methods, internet marketers quickly understood that blogs are a very convenient (not to mention effective) way of reaching a wider audience, partly due to the fact that they are perhaps more used to interactivity.

This means that, as with the Amazon business model that I explained to you in Chapter Four, comments and feedback can be left by visitors your blog, which can create a sense of community. Obviously, the same can be said for people sharing and discussing bad experiences, hence the emphasis on delivering value and quality at all times.

I'm Going To Use The 'C' Word Again!

Although the whole concept of using a blog as part of a business marketing strategy is still very much at an embryonic stage, many – even traditional bricks and mortar companies – are now understanding the benefits and how creating a following can really impact their business. Offline businesses are using blogging as part of their marketing strategy because they now realise that they can spread the word about their products or services virally, and leverage the power of the internet.

By interacting with your audience you are also starting a unique kind of relationship, one that enables them to feel valued and appreciated. This type of relationship is one that can serve you well for many years to come, so this is no short-term fix. This is all about understanding that a little effort can yield huge benefits for your business, as well as your customers.

Doing this consistently not only allows you to become respected, seen as a leading authority in your field and someone who actually cares about delivering value, help and interacting, but it continues to put you and your name out there, all-the-while increasing your digital footprint.

You will also be seen as someone who is transparent and honest, and by getting to know *you* better you will gain more trust.

In my opinion, this is one thing that holds so many businesses back and yet it is relatively simple to implement. As you've already seen, there are many ways to enhance your credibility and yet most do not use the assets that they have to do just that.

We live in an era and an ultra-competitive environment and as consumers we are perhaps more weary and skeptical than ever before of the people we do business with or buy from.

Therefore, don't you think that being more transparent, putting yourself out there, reassuring your audience about your expertise is, and offering to help or add value with no strings attached might be beneficial?

Do You Ever Feel Overwhelmed?

Simple, cumulative steps can profoundly increase the profile, reputation and in turn, the profitability of your business, but beware of something called paralysis by analysis, which can then lead to that dreaded killer of ideas, ambitions, productivity and dreams: procrastination.

For some business owners – as it is in life – sometimes there's a feeling of having to get everything done all at once, rather than breaking it down in to manageable chunks. This is actually a common problem, particularly as many business owners feel that because it's their business, they should be doing everything (or the vast majority of things) associated with it. The fact is, there are only so many hours in a day and although it's *your baby*, delegation and trusted employees and partners are there to help you.

There is a great, visual analogy that describes this type of scenario perfectly: "how do you eat an elephant?" The answer being "one mouthful at a time." And whilst you may be thinking it sounds unrealistic, I can assure you from my own experience that breaking things down *really does* help, and so I highly recommend you do it. You will become more productive and consistently tick more daily items off your to-do list.

So, the close out this chapter, what have you learned about blogging? First and foremost, it allows you and your business to provide more value to your audience, something I've rambled on about countless times already, but it's a core belief that I feel very strongly about.

Secondly, it's not as hard as you think. Just like the other strategies in this book, it simply takes a little planning, investment of time (or money if you'd prefer to outsource it) and a desire to do it.

And finally, it's a platform where you can share everything from what's happening in the industry and your opinions on any topical issues, to the do's and don'ts in your sector and your latest product launch.

But ultimately, I want you to feel inspired to go out there and do it, to make a difference – to your business and your audience.

Chapter Nine:

How The Power Of Press Releases Can

Crush Your Competitors

I first learned about the power of using press releases in 2005, during a 30-minute interview with a former car dealership General Manager and now internet marketing genius. He is someone that I studied a lot in my early years of online marketing. His name is Mike Filsaime.

Mike is highly successful at what he does, and earns millions of dollars every year from his portfolio of online businesses. Given his background and his accomplishments, he's someone worth listening to. By the way, if you haven't heard of him, simply Google his name and you will see exactly what I mean.

Press releases, if used strategically, can be an excellent way to create the right publicity for your business. Such is the speed at which news can travel, that in some cases you could be seeing your story travel right across the globe in next to no time at all.

What Exactly Is A Press Release?

A press release (or news release as it is also known) is simply a newsworthy article or white paper that is written in a 'journalistic' style. Often 200 to 500 words in length (although this really can vary), they generally should focus on a particular story relating to your business.

Now before you start worrying, you don't need to have studied journalism to be able to do this. There are however, some basic parameters that you must adhere to, some things that you can do, and some things that you cannot do. All will be revealed during the course of the next few pages.

Essentially what you want your press release to achieve is to outline a relevant or interesting story about your company or your industry. The news should be both pertinent and timely, as this is the essence of a new release.

Although what we're discussing here is using a press release as a marketing tool, it should not be a blatant sales message without any substance. The purpose of writing a press release is to highlight what is newsworthy and interesting about your company or industry, just like any other story you would read about in the press.

I suppose it's almost a stealth tactic to getting your business noticed – not quite a Trojan Horse, but much the same as all the other strategies in this book, the key is adding value – in this case: news.

So how do you get started? Well, in a similar way to what we discussed in Chapter Seven, where you can submit articles to specific websites where they can be published for people to read, the same applies with press releases. There are many specific news release sites where your story can be submitted, with many of them free, although there are some good quality paid options too. And who knows, having sent your press release to the relevant online (PR.com and PRLog.org to name a few) directories, there may be a chance that the local, national or international media end up getting hold of your story.

Of course – and let's be realistic here – it very much depends on the relevance, impact, importance and newsworthiness of your story, but you may be surprised at what can be achieved. International coverage as you would imagine would be the most difficult to achieve, however national and in particular local coverage can have a real impact on your business. It may also impact the local community too, so do not underestimate the effect of this.

In fact, let me give you a real life example of what I did for one of my clients. I am deliberately using this particular one in this example given the industry they operate in – one that is certainly very niche.

The business in question was a funeral director. Whilst this may not be near the top of your list when you're thinking about groundbreaking and newsworthy sectors, this only serves the emphasis the power of this media.

For reasons of confidentiality, I can't name the client, but having written and submitted the story, we both waited to see if any journalists, locally, nationally or internationally would bite on the story?

If the truth be known, I am not even sure my client was really expecting anything to happen, having never really had any positive news coverage before.

The Domino Effect Takes Place

Within a matter of days – less than a week after I had submitted the press release – my client had secured an interview with a local newspaper and had also been featured on a high visibility news page on their website. Not a bad result for starters and certainly an instant ROI for my client.

But the momentum was building up. There was more to come. Much more.

As the story gathered pace, the viral effect that can sometimes be caused by the internet began to kick in. A few days later my client called me again, this time to tell me he had now been asked to do a radio interview on not one, but two local radio stations, giving him the opportunity to convey his story to a completely different audience. And it didn't end there. The story continued spread further, and was also featured on a well respected, industry specific blog.

All of this was the result of one strategically crafted press release. Given the nature of the business in question – which is not exactly mainstream – it speaks volumes for how effective they can be. Needless to say my client was quite happy with this result too.

And before you think that this was a bit of a one-off, this result is not untypical. It is certainly more than possible to have your own story picked up by a variety of interested parties over a variety of media, *if* the story is positioned in the right way.

Depending on the type of press release distribution services you use, you can also have the option of having your story distributed to specific local and nationally contacts. This means your press release is sent to relevant local and national journalists to see if they're interested, and so increases the chances of your story being seen, and eventually published.

Alternatively, and this requires more sweat equity but

can also work like gangbusters, you (or one of your staff) could even search for the contact names of local business journalists and contact them with a story to see if they're interested. Journalists are generally very receptive to stories coming to them as it saves them time and effort.

What this means for you is, as my client experienced, your story may hit the traditional printed news sector, which would be a great result in itself whether this was through a local newspaper, industry magazine or with one of the national papers.

Given the power of the internet – and with many news sites having a heavy digital presence – it is just as likely to feature online too, so you'll get a double whammy. And as my client discovered, once the story is 'out there' it could soon end up on a radio station, blog or other news driven website.

So a bit like planting a seed – with a bit of thought, planning, care and attention – it could turn into something sizable. It may not work every time – and may not produce a home run every time – but the results you can achieve with a small amount of effort are certainly worth it.

Another Building Block For Your Credibility

An ongoing theme throughout this book is the 'C' word. You might be sick of the sight of it, or feel I'm placing too much emphasis on it, but I can assure you, the long-term benefits of doing this correctly are huge.

Think about each piece of activity within each of the strategies I've mapped out so far as pieces of a puzzle. You start off with a blank tabletop to begin with, but each week you add to it, little by little. A video here, a podcast there. You start blogging once a week and decide to send an article and press release once a month. It starts to add up.

But many never see the transformative effects because they're looking for instant results – the famed silver bullet – and as yet, I'm yet to find one. I'm presuming by the very fact that you're reading this book and that you've got this far, that you're different.

I'm sure by now you're starting to understand the significance and competitive advantage that can be gained here. Whether it's a press release, blog, article, video, podcast or whatever else you decide to do, it can propel your business to new heights. It does take effort, but that's one of the reasons why the majority of businesses are just about keeping their heads above water.

The question is, are you going to follow the crowd? Or are you going to chart your own destiny?

Chapter Ten:

Why Using Email Marketing Can Save And

Make You Money Simultaneously

Our journey in this book is almost complete. And just for you, I saved my favourite – and possibly the most powerful – until last.

If you were able to use a strategy today that you could save you money on the one hand, and make you money on the other, would you start using it? A rhetorical question I know.

Email marketing sometimes gets a bad reputation – much the same as its offline cousin, what is known as 'direct mail'. You may know it more affectionately as 'junk mail.'

But both are essentially forms of direct marketing, and whilst it can be perceived as a nuisance, as junk mail – or in the case of emails, as spam – it's all about using some of the principles you read early on this book – getting the right message to the right audience.

This Is The Ultimate Challenge

Once you've established those parameters, perhaps the biggest challenges in direct marketing is getting your letter or email opened by its recipient. The fact is, it doesn't matter how beneficial your product or service is, how good your offer is or even how well written the letter (or in this case your email) is, if it doesn't get opened, the contents are irrelevant.

Before we get into the nuts and bolts of email marketing, I want to touch on how some of the original principles of this were created – direct mail. There are many tried and tested creative ways to have someone open your letter, and guy I learned a tremendous amount from in this arena is Dan Kennedy.

He's a seasoned veteran and not just a direct mail expert, but a marketing magician and someone who I can definitely give credit to for my success in helping companies to achieve great results. Legend is an often over-used word, but in this case I feel that it is more than justified.

I have read many of Dan's books several times such is the passion that I have for his work. I believe they're the type of books that you can read over and over again and continue to learn new ideas, strategies and concepts.

If you are – or have been thinking about – using direct mail for your business, you can purchase or rent lists of businesses or consumers that match a variety of relevant data that fits the profile of those you are trying to target. It may be that you are focusing your efforts geographically, or perhaps you're using another or several other demographics.

However, when it comes to email marketing, I have a message so important, that it's in bold text:

You should not do this very same thing with email marketing. Not ever.

This is because in essence, you'll be spamming – basically emailing without the recipients consent.

The Can Spam Act of 2003 clearly states that it's illegal to sell – and therefore as a consequence, buy – email addresses. And although it is technically *legal* to rent a list, I still believe you're sailing close to the wind because ultimately you don't have anyone's permission to email, so I really don't recommend it.

And anyway, consider this: For the companies out there who may rent (or sell) you email lists, the email addresses are likely to have such low response rates due of the number of times they have already been bombarded with unwanted communications that it's not a good way to introduce your company to someone.

So How Do You Do It?

It's the next logical question, isn't it? Just *how* do you get people on to your email list to begin with?

The answer is you bribe them! ... ethically of course. And although I've used the word 'bribe' slightly tongue-in-cheek, what I mean is – and it's another ongoing theme in this book – you deliver value.

There are many ways you can do this, of course, but regardless of the mechanic you use, it's all about offering a reason or incentive for someone to give you their name and email address (amongst other things). This is what I was referring to in Chapter Seven as signing up. It is often referred to as opting in too, because what they are doing is opting in to your database.

You could have a special offer or free gift. Perhaps a series of videos or subscription to your newsletter? Whatever the 'hook' it should genuinely be useful, educational and enrich the life or business of those you're targeting – after all, you're expecting some commitment from them in giving you their contact details.

Once they have given you their details, your prospect can then give you *their* permission for you to send further emails (technically known as double-opt in) and this ensures you have obtained their details in compliance with the Can Spam Act. Once you have their permission, you can begin sending regular emails, perhaps a newsletter or some tips, and so you start to develop a relationship with them.

Standing Out In A
Cluttered Inbox

As I have previously mentioned, this scenario is no different whether you're using email or direct mail, and so this is a challenge that has existed for many years. The great news is that because it's been around since the dawn of advertising, there are solutions that have been honed and developed over many years that you can deploy.

Easily the most important component of all: get your email opened.

As with all successful print advertisements, direct mail pieces and something that newspapers and magazines are really great at – the key to attracting a reader's attention lies with the headline.

And it's no different with an email. It is therefore critical that you ensure your subject lines are compelling, arouse curiosity and have your readers wanting to know more.

Apart from the name of the sender, the subject line is the next most important aspect of an email. Obviously when you know the sender (particularly a close friend, family member or one of your staff), the trust element kicks in, and so regardless of the subject line you're likely to open it.

As a business, you may not (yet) have the benefit of trust, and given the vast amount emails we all receive on a daily basis, it makes perfect sense to make your subject line interesting or intriguing. Ideally it should be immediately obvious that what they've received is beneficial, or so compelling and intriguing that they should want to open it immediately. And if they don't open it immediately, what you want is for the subject line to bug them for the rest of the day so they eventually crumble and feel they have to open it.

Disclaimer: There is a potentially thin line that you shouldn't cross however. It is not about 'tricking' your intended audience, as misleading is a tactic often used by those who spam inboxes. It is not about deceiving your audience, it is about being creative whilst having something of value for them, whether it is a newsletter, an offer or something else that they might be interested in.

This is where you'll be utilising one of the core marketing principals that really hasn't changed at all in more than a century – deploying an irresistible headline, or in this case, subject line.

A Word Of Caution

You do need to be very careful with some of the words that you use in the subject line of an email. In fact, the same rules apply within the body of the email too, and this is something that I'll cover in more detail in just a moment.

Don't use over-exaggerated or hyped-up text that could possibly be misconstrued or considered as spam. This actually includes some non-aggressive, everyday words such as 'free', 'guaranteed', and 'save £'s'. Using these words might send your email to the junk folder – the equivalent of a letter being lost by Royal Mail.

Most specialist email software packages do give you guidance on this. Once you have typed your email and saved it (so before you have sent it to anyone) it will be given a rating based upon previous experiences of email deliverability. This rating will instantly let you know whether or not the email may or may not be considered as spam, and you can therefore change some of the wording of your email if necessary.

Once you've successfully delivered an email into your reader's inbox, *and* it has been opened, you must continue to keep their attention. My advice at this stage is to get straight to the point. You cannot afford to waste people's time with long, drawn out stories, certainly not in the beginning of the 'relationship' anyway.

That doesn't mean you should be brash or appear rushed, however. Just be clear and concise. A big lesson that I have learned from the very best is that you do need to tell your readers exactly what you want them to do – whether it's watch my video, subscribe to my podcast or check out this special offer. Do not be subtle about it and do not assume they'll just go ahead and do it – give them a little encouragement.

Another important part of this is that you also need to write to your reader about the things that *they* will be interested in, and not write about the areas that *you* are interested in. This may sound obvious, but I see it time and time again.

For example, if you are introducing a new product or service, then you should really be writing about the benefits that will apply to your audience. Any time someone receives a promotional communication, they're thinking about that famous radio station: WIIFM – What's In It For Me!

So you should always try and put yourself in the position of your customer or prospect, and attempt to see things from their perspective. Ultimately all they want to know is what does this mean for them and how does it benefit them.

Mind Your Language

This is an interesting one and something that I think

you'll both appreciate and be relieved about at the same time. It is a common misconception that any type of business communication, should be written using perfect Queen's English with flawless grammar.

The truth is that it really using degree-level English language grammar isn't a life or death situation. I'm sure most English lecturers, teachers or graduates may cringe at the thought of this and disagree with me, and it probably goes against everything that you've ever learned about marketing or advertising.

Now before you think that it is ok to just 'throw' something together, I should add this. Spelling **is** important. You shouldn't have copy that's littered with typos as this is going to give your company an unprofessional image. Grammar however, is less of an issue. It's always a good idea to write as you speak, that way your communications will have a nice conversational tone to them.

I'm not suggesting for one minute that you go all out and use masses of local, colloquial terms and phrases here, but as long as what you write flows nicely and is easily understood, you've achieved your goal.

If you have clients overseas, you should be thinking about how you word and phrase your communications to ensure that a clear message is understood by your reader. Things can get 'lost in translation' very easily – particularly when English isn't someone's first language – something that I experienced from working both in Europe and in the Middle East.

Another consideration could be your target audience's occupation or background, particularly if you're in the B2B arena and work with specific niches of clients.

Say you have three different groups of clients: lawyers, construction workers and second-hand car salesmen. You might want to tailor your message to each so that it better reflects their style.

I'm sure the type of conversations that take place on a construction site would differ to those in a law practice and a car dealership. So having your message resonate with your audience as much as possible is for me, a no brainer.

Also, where possible, try to avoid using jargon, too. The more simply you communicate the more likely your audience is going to understand you. An exception could be if you operate in a particularly technical field where your clients expect and enjoy reading technical terminology and acronyms. Perhaps they are fundamental part of your business, in which case this is fine.

You want to speak your audience's language, after all. But if in doubt, err on the side of caution.

Once You Track You'll
Never Look Back

One critical element in all digital marketing is tracking and measuring the effectiveness of messages and campaigns.

The great news is that many software packages do now enable you to see how many emails were delivered successfully, how many were opened, and whether some type of action was taken – clicking on a link, for example.

Of course, results will vary depending on factors such as your target audience, length and strength of relationship, and the types/prices of the products and services involved.

So, what does a successful email or campaign look like? Well, once again it does vary from industry to industry, but here's my view: If you're getting upwards of a 15 per cent open rate – people who are opening the email – and a three per cent click through rate or better – then you're on the right track.

Let me quickly explain click through rate, which you'll often see abbreviated to CTR. It's often a great idea to include a link in your emails to direct your audience to your website, blog, YouTube channel etc, where you can continue the conversation from the email, add more value, demonstrate something or sell.

And by testing different messages, lengths of emails, types of subject lines, etc, you can start to gauge what your audience is responding to. Good idea, right?

You can then begin to develop a picture of what working well and what isn't, and patterns will emerge that you can focus on, improve and work towards achieving double-digit response rates from your email marketing activity.

One Time Marketing Is Doomed

And whether a particular person in your database responds favourably or not to an email, you should have some kind of follow-up strategy lined up. It will most likely (and indeed should) differ depending on whether they *did* respond or not, with subsequent emails all working towards having them take the desired action. This doesn't need to be overly complex, but it does require a little thought and you should map out the sequence of what you want to achieve from each communication.

That very point highlights why it is critical to have a preplanned strategy, as opposed to doing something like this 'on the fly' or in an ad hoc fashion. If you have a system in place you can just set it and leave it, with emails being sent out automatically at predetermined times based on the actions of the recipient. Once you have enough data to analyse you can start to create metrics for your campaign to help achieve your objectives.

It is also worth bearing in mind that people don't open, read or respond to emails for a multitude of reasons. Perhaps they're busy, on holiday or didn't see the email as it ended up in their junk folder. Yes, they may not be interested (yet) also, but this is why following up is so crucial.

If there's one thing I learned early on in my career, it's that a prospect often has to read or hear your messages several times of more before they begin to trust you. So persistence is critical, but in a nice way – the last thing you want is to come across as desperate.

What you should not be doing is sending all of your follow up emails in the space of a week or two, as this will more than likely annoy your prospect. You want to keep drip-feeding valuable messages and interesting content, and then eventually they may start to read, listen... and act.

Following up with prospects, and especially following up with customers, is certainly a secret to the success of many businesses I know. In fact it is in itself a kind of analogy for life and business – never giving up. However, it's all about how you do it.

It's Now Time To Apply What You've Learned

In fact as I bring this chapter and this book to a close, this raises a very important point that has been mentioned more than several times in previous chapters, but it's worth mentioning one more time. You have to deliver value. Value produces trust which can produce positive results – and ultimately sales.

Yes you need to overtly sell sometimes as sales bring you revenue that helps you continue as a business. But everyone has such an overwhelming abundance of choice these days that you need to build strong relationships and be memorable. People also have high expectations and little loyalty, therefore if a brand fails to deliver they will move to one of your competitors.

Most us hate being sold to, but we enjoy being entertained, engaged and learning new things. Look for avenues to communicate your value in the right place and at the right time.

And listen to your customers. With social media, blogging and YouTube allowing comments and interaction, this is much easier than it has ever been before. Your customers – in fact anyone who's interacting with you online – will tell you what they like and don't like and this will give you valuable feedback and ideas.

So a new revolution is upon us. And in my opinion it's going to have as significant an impact as it's predecessors.

The introduction of steam engine changed the way goods and materials were transported. Horses and manpower had their limitations and now were no longer required – and as a result, greater quantities of haulage could be transported more quickly over land using steam power. Ships no longer had to rely on the wind and the extra weight they could now carry was offset by the power of its new steam engine.

Manufacturing underwent a transformation through the industrial revolution. The coal used to power steam engines was also used to make iron. In turn, iron was used to manufacture tools, improve machinery and build larger more robust construction, such as bridges.

And then there is the digital revolution, which I believe is set to leave a similar footprint in history. Suddenly information that took hours to research can be located in seconds. Purchasing items can be done in an instant. Communication and connection around the world is free. Businesses have more opportunity than at any point in history. Ignore it at your peril.

Resources

This resource section gives you information relating to some of the key people and resources that have been mentioned throughout the two sections and ten chapters of this book. In the case of a resource or a person being mentioned multiple times, the first point of reference only is featured in this section.

Section One

Facebook: Arguably the most popular of the many social networking sites on the internet today. Facebook was founded by Mark Zuckerberg whilst he was at Harvard University, along with college pals Eduardo Saverin, Dustin Moskovitz and Chris Hughes.

Yellow Pages: Used all around the world – although a dying breed – it is a telephone directory of business listings that are divided into categories according to the products and services provided.

Chapter Four

Myspace: Was the number one ranked social networking site (in terms of monthly unique visitors) until Facebook came along and overtook it in early 2008. Myspace is owned by Rupert Murdoch's News Corp Digital Media and is based in Beverly Hills in the USA.

Twitter: Created in 2006, Twitter enables you to undertake social networking by using what are called "tweets" - these are essentially text based posts of up to 140 characters that your subscribers (known as followers) can view. Think of it as a cross between texting and blogging.

Amazon: Amazon.com Inc. started trading online in 1995, primarily as a bookstore to begin with. Realising the opportunities that lay ahead, Jeff Bezos who founded the company began to diversify in terms of both its products and its markets. Amazon now sells countless items to its customers (pay a visit to their site to see what I mean!) and at the last count has seven established country-specific websites, in the USA, the UK, Canada, France, Germany, Japan and China.

Chapter Five

iTunes: A free application that can be used with a standard PC as well as an Apple Mac. It enables you to organise and play digital music and videos on your computer, as well synchronising it with your iPod, iPhone and Apple TV.

Chapter Six

YouTube: The video sharing website featured its first video in April 2005, and has gone from strength to strength since then. The company's first headquarters were above a pizzeria and Japanese restaurant in San Mateo, California, and just 18 months later it was bought by Google for a reported $1.65 billion. It now operates as a subsidiary part of the Google empire.

Google: Founded in late 1998 by Larry Page and Sergey Brin when both were studying at Stanford University, the company started life in a friend's garage in Menlo Park, California, but is now located at a state of the art facility in Mountain View, California. The company has grown exponentially from its original incorporation, with many services available now in addition to its famous search engine.

Alexa: Now part of Amazon, but was originally founded in 1996 to provide insight into web browsing behaviour. Their website, Alexa.com ranks websites on a number of criteria such as number of visitors, page views per user, the time spent on the website and certain demographic data, to name but a few.

Chapter Seven

Yahoo!: Located in the famous Silicon Valley in Sunnyvale, California, Yahoo! Inc. is perhaps most notably known for its search engine, web portal and email service. Yahoo! Inc. was founded by electrical engineering graduates from Stanford University Jerry Yang and David Filo in 1994.

MSN Search: It was in late 1998 that Microsoft launched its MSN Search facility. Over the course of the next 11 years several changes were made by Microsoft, culminating in the creation of Bing (see below) in the Summer of 2009.

Bing: The result of several changes and improvements to their existing search engines, Microsoft launched Bing to enhance a user's search experience. Most notably, Bing will sort your search into categories that can often throw up very useful additions to your search.

Chapter Eight

Gareth Harries' blog: My friend, Gareth Harries traveled around the world, compiling an entertaining blog whilst on his travels, in often rather challenging circumstances. You can see his blog at www.travelblog.org/Bloggers/GWK1/

Chapter Nine

Mike Filsaime: An author, software developer, renowned speaker, personal and business coach and most of all – an intensive marketer. Mike has exponentially grown and developed his company, Mike Filsaime Inc. in just 6 short years, and now occupies a 5,500 square feet office and has 17 employees and 18 virtual employees. You can visit his website at www.MikeFilsaime.com.

Chapter Ten

Dan Kennedy: He is in my opinion, one of *the* best marketers of our generation and a huge influence on my own career. A provocative, truth-telling author of seven popular books and thirteen business books in total, at the time of writing this book. Dan is a successful, multi-millionaire entrepreneur, trusted marketing advisor, consultant and a coach to hundreds of private entrepreneurial clients. You can visit his website at www.DanKennedy.com and free information is available at www.NoBSBooks.com.

About The Author

Simon Thurston is a business and marketing coach for small and medium sized businesses, who improves the sales revenue and profitability of the companies that he works with, through a variety of proven methods. He has also studied and worked with some of the biggest names in the industry.

In terms of his education, Simon gained a Business Studies, Accountancy and Law Diploma from the Royal Forest of Dean College in the UK. He would then go on to graduate from the widely renowned Business School at the University of Wolverhampton in the UK, where he obtained an Honours Degree in Business, Marketing, Information Technology and Languages.

Simon has also had experience of working with overseas companies. He spent time in the South of France, working with the famous Université Stendhal in Grenoble, in the heart of the Alps. He also lived in Saudi Arabia for two years, where he was able to work with one of the largest and most successful privately owned conglomerates in the country.

He firmly believes in constantly learning and helping others to do the same. Simon is also an advocate of the power of positive thinking, personal and self-development and philanthropy, where he supports several charitable organisations in the UK.

www.ingramcontent.com/pod-product-compliance
Lightning Source LLC
Chambersburg PA
CBHW071223050326
40689CB00011B/2433